THE
Old Photographs
SERIES

AROUND
BOLSOVER

A Market Place birds eye view, taken from the Cross Keys. Buildings now gone include the Coop, police station, Woodhead's and not forgetting the petrol pumps which to many seemed as permanent as Mrs. Eyre's cycle business which stood alongside them.

THE
Old Photographs
SERIES

AROUND
BOLSOVER

Compiled by
Bernard Haigh

CHALFORD

BATH • AUGUSTA • RENNES

First published 1994
Copyright © Bernard Haigh, 1994

The Chalford Publishing Company Limited
St Mary's Mill, Chalford, Stroud
Gloucestershire GL6 8NX

ISBN 07524 0021 5

Typesetting and origination by
Alan Sutton Limited
Printed in Great Britain by
Redwood Books, Trowbridge

Erratum: *magnesium* on back cover text should read *magnesian*.

Castle Street before the gas lamp in the Market Place was replaced by the war memorial. The drainage channel down the centre of the road leads to the parish pump now gone, as has the handsome ivy covered building where the electricity showroom now stands. To the right all has been demolished except the Anchor.

Contents

Acknowledgements

The enthusiasm of local people for a third collection of old photographs of Bolsover and district and their subsequent loan of previously unpublished material has made this book possible.

In particular I wish to thank:

Granville Spray, Freda Kitchen, Grace and Les Hewitt, Phyllis Bird, Roy Madin, Alan James, Mrs. J. Poulter, Cliff Paulson, Rita Inns, Charles and Bunty Margerrison, Bolsover Civic Society, Mrs. K. Taylor, Maureen and Gordon Caley, George Poulter, Betty Ashby, Mary and Mrs. E. Spray, Betty Hunter, Dorothy Ford, Carol Hayes (for typing the mss), Marion Whitehead, Mrs. E. Parsons, Julie Hulme, Bessie and Les Holmes, Sue and Les Coulton, Mervyn Sanders, F. Allfree, Pam Ashley, Joan Moorcroft, Betty Swain.

As always Jeanette, my wife, encouraged me and ensured I had the opportunity to compile the collection. Rachel and Thomas helped with the layout.

Finally, I would like to dedicate the book to Oscar Coupe, a man whose knowledge of past Bolsover life is unsurpassed and who over the years has been so generous in sharing this information.

Introduction

Ten years ago in 'Bolsover Remembered' I revealed to a rather surprised local readership that within a space of six months Bolsover had been compared not only to 'some lovely hill town in Tuscany' but also as 'a gem of landscape and composition'. The first statement was made by Derbyshire writer and broadcaster Roy Christian in an article for 'Derbyshire Life and Countryside' and the second by a Sunday Observer reporter in an article entitled rather unoriginally 'Skinner's Stronghold'. Locally we accepted such extravagant praise in a dismissive, no nonsense, north Derbyshire way little realising the seeds were being sown for a sea change in Bolsover's way of life.

At the same time as we were being written about in the glossy 'Sundays' and in the County magazine, a watershed in British industrial life was shaking not only Bolsover but the whole country. The 1984—5 miners strike was dividing families, coalfields, unions and the nation in a way unparalleled since the days of the depression and the general strike sixty years earlier. Not even during the 1979 'winter of discontent' had local and national passions been stirred so radically and for mining communities so tragically. The end of the strike signalled the beginning of the end for deep coal mining throughout Britain, and Bolsover like so many similar communities was going to have to come to terms with a fundamental change in its economic and social base.

In retrospect it is easy to identify a point in time that signalled the sea change. At the time it was not so obvious but the great shift was now underway which would transform Bolsover.

Ten years later, with Bolsover on the threshold of a new coal less age what now; commuter town, tourist mecca or yet another former mining community confused as to how it should set out its stall for the future. It would seem appropriate to celebrate its recent past in photographs.

Yet, as can be seen within these pages Bolsover was not built exclusively on coal. It has a history as a major Derbyshire settlement going back to 1155 when William Peveril built his royal castle perched high on the escarpment.

Late in the seventeenth and early eighteenth centuries Charles Cavendish, youngest son of that indefatigable Derbyshire matriarch Bess of Hardwick, started to build a castle which today, with its flamboyant architecture and incomparable position, echoes a Disney fantasy. Round the gates of the Cavendish mansion and following the medieval linear street pattern were erected cottages and farm houses, a few of which still remain on High Street, Church Street and Market Place. Charles I and his Queen, Henrietta Maria were entertained here by the Duke of Newcastle, for which event Ben Jonson wrote his dramatic masque 'Love's Welcome to Bolsover'. This must have been magical when performed in such a setting.

The area did possess some small scale industries and crafts, pottery, stone quarrying, buckle and spur making and of course arable farming, the town being surrounded to the north and east by productive agricultural land. But this period of activity in the Bolsover scene was short lived. As the Cavendish family married into the Bentincks and the Dukes of Portland forsook Bolsover for Welbeck Abbey the castle slept, taking on the image of a lifeless ruin. Bolsover itself reverted to its position as a former market town on the road to nowhere in particular.

Like any self respecting beauty, Bolsover slept for well over one hundred years until 1889 when the Bolsover Colliery Company sank its shafts on the side of the river Doe Lea and proceeded to transform the town on the hill and the countryside down in the valley. The population grew tenfold to ten thousand people, importing labour from Wales, Durham, Lancashire and Staffordshire. At New Bolsover the company built a colliery model village, architecturally probably one of the most important in the country. They helped create a network of mineral and passenger railway lines down in the valley, dug clay holes for brickworks and ensured that the Duke of Portland became one of the richest men in the country. The old town up on the hill grew with nonconformist chapels, miners welfares, red brick terraces, schools, an Urban District Council and gradually a valuable sense of community which remains today. Much of this is depicted within these pages.

However, this book is not just Bolsover town. Its surrounding villages have each retained their separate identities. In the case of Shuttlewood and Carr Vale ribbon development connects them to the larger community. Palterton and Scarcliffe are still agricultural settlements with farms,a grand eighteenth century house in each and some pretty cottages intermingling with the commuter in fill. There has been less change here although Scarcliffe has sacrificed some picturesque cottages below the church and a fine manor house. Memories of Sutton Hall have been included as an important record of a grand house, but today a rather sad ruin. It was saved from almost certain destruction by the presence of mind of Sir Osbert Sitwell at nearby Renishaw. The house is as much a part of an extended Bolsover as are Palterton or Shuttlewood. Although a mere two miles away as the crow files across the Scarsdale valley stand on any part of the escarpment and Sutton Hall peers blindly across to the castle. In early morning with the sun on its honey coloured walls the palladian frontage presents a truly magnificent site.

If it is true that the past mirrors the future, we have little cause for concern at what awaits these former coalfield communities. The photographs show people working together whether it is coping with disasters at Carr Vale, helping in soup kitchens during the terrible years of the depression, chapel anniversaries, flower fairs and galas, May day gatherings or amateur dramatics. There is less of this type of activity today but the community is a settled one with an inbuilt village friendliness, surprising outsiders used to a more insular way of life.

The physical fabric of the town is changing. Ten years ago concern was expressed about many town centre sites and the future of particular buildings. Since then the Parish Church is in a more settled physical state, a supermarket has filled a derelict site in Town End and the Cooperative Society is currently building on perhaps the most important central position of all. Down in the valley New Bolsover has been given a tasteful facelift although the green remains worthy of more attention. Ponds, walkways and even new orchards have been created by the local groundwork trust and the valley enterprise park is set to expand on the colliery site. Perhaps most important of all the local district council, now by far the single largest employer of labour in the town, has centralised its offices in Bolsover, offering the greatest potential yet for local employment and a spending power of three hundred people which is certain to benefit the local economy.

Perhaps at such a time of change and renewal it is pertinent to examine life as it was. The following pages record that time.

Bernard Haigh

One
Street Scenes

Looking from the church gates down Church Street towards Cotton Street it is difficult to recognise the same view today. The house to the right is now the doctor's surgery followed by the post office. Crossing Cotton Street is a portion of Middle Street which no longer exists; it is merely a flight of steps and an archway through to the old Market Place. To the left we have the cottages where the library now stands.

A Turn of the century High Street scene when the road still boasted quite a few handsome Georgian houses. The two at the Langwith Road end have now gone as has the white painted building beyond the Blue Bell. All eyes are fixed on the photographers, even the horse and cart remains stationary. A pity someone didn't tell the gentleman in the centre that his face would be lost to posterity.

A fine hearse, owned by R. & E. Marsh whose haulage, carriage and removal business was based at Moorfield Mews at the junction of Moor Lane and Town End. A building which looks fairly unchanged today. Bob Marsh was one of the first in Bolsover to acquire Ford lorries for his haulage business.

This row of cottages stood at the corner of High Street and Hornscroft Road; the corner of the churchyard is to the right. Taken in the 1940s some of the windows have been 'modernised' with casements, others retain their Yorkshire sliding sashes. A very harmonious row with their weathered red pantiled roofs and rough cast magnesian limestone.

The Barley Mow public house or the 'old thatch' as it was more popularly known stood gable end on to Hill Top in the corner of what is now the Assembly Hall car park. In this photograph it awaits demolition and the thatched roof has been replaced by corrugated iron panels.

This photograph from 1860 and the one opposite show what was perhaps the finest Georgian house in Bolsover and the most interesting and historic of its many pubs. Both buildings, which stood in the Market Place, are now alas demolished. The butchers adjoined the White Swan and the old pub pre dated the present building. The butchers, minus the ornate Victorian ironwork was originally a farm house of grand design. The pub was a cruck building from ground level to roof, with cross beams carrying the first floor. It was demolished in 1926 but part of the original stone was used after cleaning and squaring for building the pub we see today. Manorial courts were held here regularly until 1926.

A closer view of Gregory's marvellously ornate wrought iron shop frontage.

The vicious looking implements belonged to Mr. A. Flecknell whose shop was opposite the war memorial in the Market Place. His display offers a very novel way of filling a butchers shop window on closing day. Mr. Flecknell was originally named Fleischner but changed to the more anglicised Flecknell during the 1914–18 war when anti German feeling was at its height. The enterprising butcher owned a second shop at Carr Vale. One of his brothers was the postmaster at Palterton.

To be sold by
AUCTION,
By Mr. Shacklock,
ON MONDAY THE SIXTH DAY OF APRIL, 1818,
AT THE GATE PUBLIC HOUSE, IN PALTERTON,

In the County of Derby,

THE HOUSEHOLD
Furniture,
BREWING VESSELS, &c.

THE PROPERTY OF MR. W. MOTTERSHAW,

CONSISTING OF

ONE dozen and half of chairs ; four long forms ; three round tables ; one large oval table ; ten good convenient sized barrels ; two mash tubs ; one gathering tub ; one cooler ; one good feather bed ; two pair of bedsteads ; four iron candlesticks ; two brass candlesticks ; half a dozen knives and forks ; four spittoons ; a quantity of pots, in lots ; water kit and tundish ; one gallon piggin ; four good plated cups ; four pewter pints, two ditto half pints, two pewter quarts, and two plated half pint measures ; a quantity of glasses, pot measures and jugs ; cast metal brewing pan, 70 gallons, with underworks nearly new ; hop sieve, brigs, and numerous other effects.

Sale to commence at Twelve o'Clock.

WOODHEAD, PRINTER, CHESTERFIELD.

In the nineteenth century auctions of property and chattels were usually held in local public houses. These two took place in 1818 at the Swan Inn, Market Place and the Gate Inn Palterton. They are fascinating historic records of the household contents of past centuries. The Bolsover auction of Mr. G. Shipstone's property contains two marvellously descriptive pieces of land; 'Rickety Rushes' at Hockley and 'Cow Smithy' under the castle.

TO BE SOLD BY

AUCTION,

BY

Mr. G. Shacklock,

AT THE HOUSE OF MR. JOHN HINDE, SWAN INN, BOLSOVER, DERBYSHIRE,

On FRIDAY,

THE THIRTEENTH OF FEBRUARY, 1818,

AT FOUR O'CLOCK IN THE AFTERNOON,

(Subject to such conditions as shall be then produced, and in the following or such other lots, as may be agreed upon at the time of sale.)

A VALUABLE COPYHOLD

Estate,

(Situate as hereinafter particularized,)

THE PROPERTY OF MR. G. SHIPSTONE,

First Lot.

A dwelling house with the barn, stable & other out buildings thereto belonging, situate in Hockley, and a close of land called the Rickety Rushes, containing two acres

Second Lot.

Two closes situate under the castle hill, called the Cow Smithys, containing altogether four acres & one rood.

☞ *The Purchaser may have Possession of the above Premises at Lady Day next.*

✲✲ *G. SHIPSTONE, will shew the Premises, of whom further particulars may be known.*

BOLSOVER, JAN. 24th 1818.

Two photographs of Bolsover baths and the Bath Superintendent's house at the bottom of Castle Lane. The first was taken as building work was progressing, the second on completion in 1925. The baths were built on land given by the Duke of Portland to the miner's welfare committee fund at a cost of £6.150. The whole scheme included public baths which could be boarded over for dances and concerts, slipper baths and showers. The stone dressing was quarried locally at Kiveton Park and with boundary wall and wrought iron gates ensured a handsome appearance. Closed in the late 1980s Bolsover baths were never replaced and an extremely important community facility lost.

Hill Top towards the Market Place. All the buildings on the right have now gone although those to the left remain virtually unchanged.

The Star Supply Stores started life in Town End, later moving into the Market Place where it occupied part of the ground floor of the magnificent Georgian house next to the White Swan. The ground floor extension with its wrought ironwork served as the shop premises. The balcony itself was used as a viewing place for Market Place processions and events.

By the looks on their faces the policemen have been caught nipping into the White Swan for a quick half! This fine cruck building was demolished in 1926. Kimberleys Brewery drew up a scheme for restoration of the building in 1915 but it was decided that alterations to the main beams and support posts would possibly result in collapse of the entire structure and so the decision was taken to demolish. Delayed for ten years by the first world war the later building is of solid if rather bland appearance. The old pub sign seen here, a coronated swan, its neck encircled by a chained crown remains above the door today.

Interesting in view of the fact that today, in 1994, these buildings between the Swan and Cavendish pubs are the latest in the town centre to be demolished for the new Cooperative Stores development. The one to the right was fronted with an astonishingly unsympathetic and ugly concrete facing, although the roof line we see here was still visible to the observant passer by. Hilton's shoe shop was for many years a permanent town centre business.

This atmospheric scene looks down Old Hill at its junction with Craggs Road towards the castle. Some of the houses to the immediate left remain but those to the right have gone. The cottage in the centre was at one time the home of Nurse Cutts, the village midwife.

A panoramic view up Langwith Road, taken from the church tower in the days before Hornscroft Road was widened by taking some of the grave yard. Prominent features include the church hall, tennis courts and Hillstown water tower.

An important view of Hockley, an area which with the widening of Station Road and the demolition of all the buildings seen here has changed totally from what can be seen on the photograph. To position the area note the Craggs towards Hill Top, immediately above the cottages on the right.

This Market Place scene was probably taken in 1924 for the funeral of Mr. James Allcock, manager of Ireland and Hartington Collieries. A very substantial member of the community who commanded a prestigious funeral.

21

Front and rear views of cottages, now demolished, on Old Hill. Built of rough cast magnesian limestone they were built for agricultural workers in the days before Bolsover became a coal town. Notice the old mangle in the back yard.

Bolsover Castle, Derbyshire.

The little castle rests behind a blanket of shrubs and ivy in this nineteenth century view. A farm gate leads to the Terrace range, shown in the bottom photograph. In the days when it was owned by the Portland family the building was regarded more for its picturesque ruin quality rather than its architectural uniqueness. The Terrace itself is almost hidden behind ivy and trailing undergrowth.

Everyone is very conscious of the camera in this Town End scene – and all are keeping their distance! Today a photographer taking the same scene would be mown down by a number 81 bus. Look at the gentleman in front of the Cavendish with his knee breeches and gaitors. Over his arm is his poachers bag – with or without a ferret?

The same scene but taken from Town End and on a different occasion. Passers by still regard the photographer as enough of a novelty to stop what they are doing and pose for the camera. Happily, ninety years on every single building seen here remains.

The focal point of this view of Castle Street towards the castle is the original Angel Inn, owned by George and Hannah Adsetts. It is highly likely that the woman outside is Hannah who also worked as a linen maid to Mrs. Hamilton-Grey at the castle. The parish pump can be seen housed in its stone shelter outside the first house to the left. The whole scene reflects the rather neglected and 'remote from anywhere' air that was pre colliery Bolsover.

Mrs. Watson stands outside Shaw's butchers shop in the Market Place, a building now housing Martin's World Travel. Very much a traditional butchers shop frontage with glazed tiles, this red brick building replaced Mason's, a butchery housed in former farm premises.

These idyllic looking cottages stood to the rear of Town End. Today they would be lovingly restored and valued as important vernacular buildings. Forty years ago lack of preservation and conservation grants signalled their eventual demolition. One cottage was occupied by Miss Emmy Stevenson, a schoolmistress in the early years of this century.

Opposite: A 1920s scene of Underwood's buses which connected Bolsover with Mansfield and surrounding villages. No. 3B travelled to Shuttlewood and Bentinck. The one behind appears to have solid tyres.

Wycherley's chemist shop, such a feature of the Market Place scene for generations of Bolsover people stands on the left hand corner with 'Cow Tail Row' curving down into Hockley. The photograph illustrates the striking geological land form on which the town stands. The deep central Hockley valley spreads downhill away from the limestone escarpment which itself run towards Shuttlewood. In the 1940s the road divided at the police station.

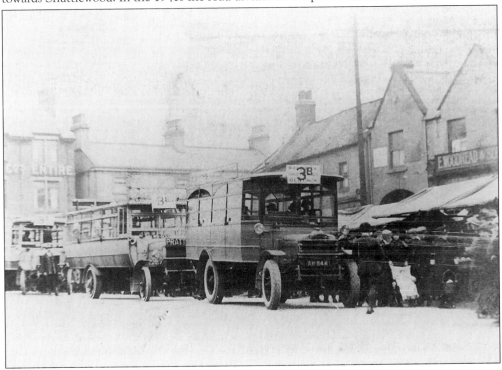

The Cavendish in the Market Place is little changed from this Edwardian photograph, although the archway is now filled in. It remains a handsome mock Elizabethan building with very confident twin central gables.

A combination of magnesian limestone with pantiled roof cottages adjoin a red brick terrace in this corner of Middle Street and Cotton Street. All now demolished.

Turn of the century Town End shows what is now Marples but was then Hinde's fish and chip shop, followed by Tom Brittain's pawn shop, a butchers and then a bakery housed in what is now Town End pharmacy.

Crossing the road the stone building first left was Mr. Pitkin's marvellous combination of blacksmith's and mechanics workshop, indicating the change over from horse to car. The two bay windowed houses adjacent were the homes of Eric Cowper, local plumber and Jack Coupe who by day was a Prudential Insurance Agent but at night a well known organiser of local concerts and dances.

The whole row of buildings on Station Road, stretching on the right towards the Market Place have now gone, although the ones to the left including the pottery and Caxton House, merely glimpsed here, remain. The Nags Head pub symbolised the fact that Hockley as this area was known was far more of a community that it is today.

The old Market Place before the war memorial supplanted the gas lamp in 1921. Greenwood's chemist has gone but Dr. Spencers house, later Kennington's the dentist and now Norman and Ludlam remains. C.H. Mason was a butcher operating from an old barn attached to the former farm house.

Middle Street: the street that no longer exists except as a street name connecting two car parks. There are no clues whatever left on the ground to tell us in which direction we are looking and to confuse further the current Middle Street has been realigned. The reality is that this is a view from Cotton Street up what is now the market steps and under the archway towards Norman and Ludlam. Every single building here is now demolished. Note the early television aerial!

The old police station with its clock divides Hockley from Hill Top. The Black Bull remains unchanged but the Assembly Hall is more isolated as the adjoining cottages are now gone.

Blind Lane was at one time a rural trackway connecting Shuttlewood Road with Woodhouse Lane. Today it still retains a rural feel but plunges towards the smoking mass of the Coalite Plant.

The Market Place in the late 1920s. The small cottage centre is now a shop and the telephone box less picturesque. Otherwise little has changed.

Hall Farm, Bolsover Woodhouse was sited on Welbeck property at the bottom of Blind Lane. Built in 1719 Mrs. K. Taylor remembers a bedroom fireplace carved with that mythical creature the griffin. The Holmes family farmed the land for many years and kept peacocks which roosted in the nearby ash tree. The house was demolished and the farmland used by Bolsover colliery for its coal waste tips.

This marvellously proportioned eighteenth century house may still be seen in the Market Place, although heavily disguised. For many years it was the home of Christopher Hinde, Secretary to Bolsover Gas Works, Registrar, Deacon and Sunday School Superintendent of the Congregational Church where he lies buried. Today the ground floor houses the vet and Tom Wragg, the nurseryman. The centre door remains but minus its flight of steps. To the first floor the sashes have been exchanged for casements.

What is now the chemist was at this time a private house with grocers adjoining (the entrance was at the far gable end). The Beehive shop frontage is now utterly dispoilt. The sign in the stonework 'Peveril House' is still there.

Looking down Town End from Moor Lane the buildings to the right belonging to Hunt's farm have now gone. The old lodging house at Church Yard Corner was a general store until the late 1970s and later converted to a private house. As a lodging house it was home to many itinerants including 'Watercress Jess' who, in season, gathered watercress from the stream flowing through Scarcliffe. This he sold for two pence a bunch to the cry of 'Fine fresh watercress'.

High Street with its zig zag cottages taken from the top of Castle Lane.

Looking down Hill Top in 1946 we see the outbuildings to Hill Top Farm, later demolished and the site used for the Hides Green development. The cottages to the left, opposite Sherwood Lodge gates have also gone.

Sherwood Lodge was built by Abel Sykes J.P., one time director of the Bolsover Colliery Company and main leaseholder of land belonging to the Duke of Portland at a time when the newly established colliery company was anxious to sink shafts on his Lordship's land. Abel Sykes therefore was an important link between the Duke and the Company. Sherwood Lodge, built in 1897, was the grandest private house in Bolsover. In 1948 it became the offices for Bolsover UDC. Today it is a small portion of the new District Council accommodation. This photograph dates from the 1950s.

At the turn of the century coal was sold by the load and not by weight. It was up to the carter to get as much as possible in his cart. O.A. Coupe appears to have done rather well!

A very satisfying look across the Hockley valley and along Hill Top. The cottages in the foreground. 'Cow Tail Row' have now gone, as have the police station, middle right and the row of cottages opposite Sherwood Lodge gates.

St. Mary's House, Castle Street, an early nineteenth century house with late Victorian octagonal bays in mock Strawberry Hill Gothic. Built by the Duke of Portland at the end of the High Street approach to the Castle Terrace range it has acted as the masters house to the adjoining church school and the residence of the Parish Church curate. Today it is privately owned and listed grade II, the only changes being the gates and boundary hedge.

Coal horses haul up Station Road one of the heaviest loads of coal it would be possible to fit into a standard sized coal cart. The steep gradient of the hill and the weight of the load demanded two stout horses.

One of the three corn mills erected in the days when Bolsover was a large agricultural village. This one known as Bagshaw's Mill, from the name of the miller, was in the 'Middle Field' on Welbeck Road. Today, the chimney has gone as have the outbuildings to the front but the main mill building has been converted into a house.

This section of Welbeck Road remains fairly unchanged although the row of houses was of more uniform appearance with standard ground floor bay windows and first floor sashes. This now rather busy corner was at the turn of the century at the end of town and very quiet.

A second view of Welbeck Road but looking left towards Town End and straight ahead where the North Star Club now stands can be glimpsed the distant spire of Hill Top chapel. The garden railings were all removed during the second world war as scrap metal for armaments but unfortunately never used or replaced. Today it would be a very foolhardy child who stood in the middle of Welbeck Road as this young lady is doing.

An interesting row of brick and slate roofed cottages on Hill Top opposite Sherwood Lodge gates. Now demolished the site provides an uninterrupted view towards the castle.

The beginning of High Street at its junction with Hornscroft and Langwith Road. The cottages and the majority of properties up to the Blue Bell have now gone.

A closer view of the fine Georgian and early Victorian houses which may be glimpsed in the previous photograph. Demolition has already started with the double fronted house and its ground floor bay standing next door to the Blue Bell. The two storey cottage adjoining the house with the ivy remains today but in a very much disguised form.

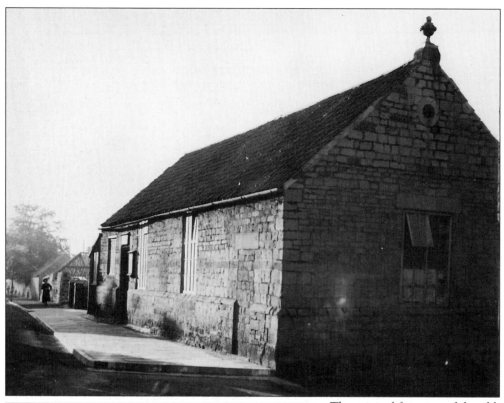

The original function of the old tithe barn at Cotton Street's junction with High Street was as a storage place for the agricultural tithe of the parish. It was later renamed the Portland Centre before the building of the Elder Citizen's hall.

Church Street leading into Middle Street.

Mrs. Ann Hardwick with grandson John outside numbers 7 and 9 High Street, in the 1930s. At this time the house which had been originally one dwelling was divided into two.

A view to the rear of two and three storey houses on Castle Street. The site is now the well landscaped car park between High Street and Castle Street.

A rather derelict looking Cotton Street, interesting because it is one of the few surviving photographs to show the street pattern of Middle Street to the left, in front of the fine high gabled stone cottage and Church Street to the right, with the post office on the corner. The library site opposite would appear to be minus its row of cottages, indicating that demolition of this area has already begun.

J.A. Lakin, grocer and general dealer is pictured outside his Town End shop, all ready to weigh out one pound of currants. Today the shop frontage remains, only the sign has changed.

Looking across the graveyard towards the Clowne road in the far distance, this 1960s view takes us up and round Welbeck Road,. Town End Chapel, Bolsover Clinic, Welbeck Road Boys and Bolsover Infants school are the landmarks in the centre of the photograph.

These two aerial views of Bolsover were taken just before the second world war and show a fairly compact town. The newest development, the right hand side of Castle Lane, (right foreground) is in the process of being built. It is interesting to see that below the terrace range to the castle there were no trees in 1939.

In this view there is no Castle Estate. Kitchen Croft is open common land (centre) and the town centre is much more crowded with buildings than today.

High Street has retained a surprisingly rural feel, even today, and this scene with the pony and trap captures it beautifully. To the left by the little boy in his sailor suit can be glimpsed the twin gables connected by a garden wall of Cuthbert's haulage business. This seventeenth century building was perhaps the most picturesque in High Street.

Len Gregory began his one man bus concern in 1926 during the general strike. He later expanded with local and regional charabanc outings and a haulage business.

Bolsover Urban District Council Election, 1919.

To the Electors of the SOUTH WARD,

Ladies and Gentlemen,

I have consented to offer myself for Election, and beg to tender the following for your consideration :—

RECORD. (1) Nearly seven years Member of the Council ; three years Chairman of the Highways Committee.

(2) Member of Food Control, and the Executive of Chesterfield Area Rationing Committees.

(3) I have always been a strong advocate of doing everything possible to improve the Public Health, and for the Council doing all the Scavenging of the District. The Council will do the Scavenging after the end of March.

(4) I have attended 249 meetings out of 255, and always worked hard for the benefit of all classes of the community.

FUTURE WORK. If elected, I will do my utmost to promote the following :—

(1) An adequate Housing Scheme, which will allow a tenant, if he wishes, to buy his house by instalments.

(2) The maintenance of the present houses in a sanitary, habitable condition.

(3) Public Baths.

(4) Restoration of Roads to their pre-war standard. (Work on them was largely stopped owing to materials being unobtainable.)

(5) Motor Bus Service to Chesterfield.

(6) Greatly improved Postal services.

(7) Ample Educational facilities to be provided by the Local Technical Committee.

(8) Ratepayers to decide, by a Referendum, whether or not the Water works shall be bought.

(9) Rearrangement of Ward Boundaries, so that all Carr Vale people shall vote together.

I make a strong appeal to each Elector, especially the women, for support. The reforms I advocate are of the most importance to the mothers and children, who have not the same chance of getting away from home as the men, and must ' carry on ' there, no matter what the conditions.

Support me, and I'll work fearlessly and conscientiously for you.

Trusting that my Experience and Work during the past, will be carefully considered.

I am, Ladies and Gentlemen,

Your Obedient Servant,

H. W. DAY,

77, Shuttlewood Road, Bolsover.

Printed & Published by Geo. KENT. Station Road, Bolsover.

The first local election to the UDC following the Armistice took place in 1919. H.W. Day's election manifesto made special appeal to the women of the ward. It is interesting that if elected he pledged to allow tenants the right to buy their council houses, seventy years before the Thatcher government's similar policy. The printing was done by Geo. Kent, Station Road who for many years was the Bolsover printer. His son Harold followed him into the business.

Two
Scarcliffe

A photograph recapturing something of the pride Station Master Hunt took in his family and his station. Alongside is his second wife, the very wasp waisted former Miss Askew and in the background the iron railway bridge which carried passengers across the Lancashire, Derbyshire and East Coast line. Taken about 1910 it could be a scene from E. Nesbit's 'The Railway Children' written at this time. The station closed in 1951.

Rose Cottage which stood below the church. Note the 'Yorkshire sash' windows on the first floor. Peculiar to northern counties the sash slides horizontally rather than vertically. Now demolished, today the cottages would be valued and regarded as vital to the village scene.

Mr. and Mrs. George Crawshaw who farmed Manor Farm. In horse and trap and taken outside a house which remains little changed.

Bernard Hodson, blacksmith at Langwith Colliery shoeing a horse in 1928. The horse and cart were used for carting coal to miners families.

Looking up Main Street with the village pump in the centre, just above the last house on the right. A very smart collection of children in Norfolk jackets and breeches, with some of the girls even wearing hats.

This very cheerful family tea, taken in high summer, shows the Mellors family of Vale House. Left to right: Miss Hollis (married John Mellors), Miss Askew (became the second wife to station master Hunt), Mrs. Elizabeth Mellors, (formerly Miss Pearson of Pearson's Potteries), Tom Mellors, Mrs. Hollis, Mrs. Tom Mellors and Mrs. Hollis (senior). The Hollis family lived in a cottage across from the church and were the owners of a fine threshing machine which travelled round the parish farms at harvest time.

The dove cote, Hall Farm; the house building may be seen to the left while to the right is the gable end to the farm yard buildings of Frank Chappell. Today only the house remains.

Jack Mellors, butcher, stands to the left of the photograph, outside his shop and home at Vale House. Billy Blacknall and Jenny Jones in the cart. The photography conveys something of the pride Jack Mellors obviously took in his business, home, staff and conveyance.

Scarcliffe village school in the 1930s. Mr. Yeomans was headmaster and church organist.

These two cottages, the homes of the gamekeeper and underkeeper were situated in Langwith woods, Scarcliffe and demolished in 1965. Taken in 1888 we see head gamekeeper Joseph Evans and his family. Left to right: the underkeeper, Annie, Bob, Arthur, Ernest and Joe Evans, Mrs. Eliza Evans with son Jack, Joseph Evans, underkeeper and Harry. Joseph was head gamekeeper from 1877 to 1895. His son Jim became head keeper in 1914, living in the same cottage as his parents until retirement in 1948 at the age of 71.

The Shaw family who owned the Horse and Groom, taken about 1912. The twin girls were born at the pub in 1906. The photograph shows the pony and trap straddled across Langwith Road. The houses to the left are still recognisably those we can see today. To the right of Mrs. Shaw may be glimpsed the distant outline of the parish church.

A scene inside the blacksmiths shop which was sited in Malthouse Yard. The blacksmith at work, shoeing a very patient horse, is George Whitworth of Palterton.

This birds eye view of Scarcliffe from the church tower shows to the bottom right a corner of the Manor House farm yard demolished by Chatsworth Estates to make way for Devonshire Cottages. Manor House tenants lived across the road, now the green. Between road and farmyard can be seen pig and hen runs belonging to the cottages. Chappell's farm buildings are immediately above those of the Manor House. Top left is Malthouse Yard with its 'L' shape of cottages.

Harry Camm of Station Farm and his very fine Cambridge roller.

Scarcliffe village in the early 1900s. Rose Cottages stand below St. Leonards Church on what is now the green.

Scarcliffe rectory is an excellent example of a small Victorian rectory, typical of thousands situated in country villages throughout Victorian and Edwardian England. Just large enough for the Rector's family with room for parish meetings and a couple of servants such buildings must have provided a comfortable lifestyle for their inhabitants. Today the rectory is in private hands and sympathetically restored.

A full view of the barns to Chappell's farm on Main Street. This fine range of magnesian limestone buildings with its magnificent roofs was demolished in the 1960s to make way for Devonshire Cottages.

Scarcliffe village scene in 1923. All the buildings seen here remain although the two cottages to the left are now one and the post office immediately above has moved across the way. The road itself is today tarmac clean but not nearly so evocative of rural life complete with mud and horse droppings.

Three

Sutton Hall

Sutton Scarsdale Hall must be one of the most majestic ruins in the country. Built in 1724 to the designs of Francis Smith of Warwick for Nicholas Leake, fourth and last Earl of Scarsdale the house in 1824 passed into the hands of the Arkwright family, descendants of Richard Arkwright inventor and industrialist. The family sold up in 1920 at a time when few people could afford the upkeep of such a property. Bought by a speculator who proceeded to sell the lead from the roof and anything else disposable the building soon lapsed into a ruinous state. The interest of Sir Osbert Sitwell at nearby Renishaw, Derbyshire County Council and eventually English Heritage has ensured that what can be saved of this magnificent pile remains.

The garden terrace with its formal planting and classical urns provides an impression of the grandness of the whole design.

The drawing room is the one room in the house to be saved. Acquired by the Philadelphia Museum of Art, Pennsylvania, U.S.A. it can still be seen to this day.

The stucco work on this saloon ceiling was almost certainly performed by Italian master craftsmen resident in England in the eighteenth century. The house had two Venetian saloons on separate floors with fireplaces at both ends.

Four
Leisure Time

For anyone over the age of forty, Sunday school anniversaries are looked upon as past highlights of the calendar. Here we see the participants of one local chapel progressing through the old Market Place towards the Congregational Church. The cart, in addition to children, conveys a piano and orange boxes courtesy of Sir Ernest Shentall. The buildings to the rear are Greenwood's chemist shop which when demolished left a 'hole' in this corner of the Market Place which still needs filling and Dr. Spencer's house which today houses Norman and Ludlam.

Bolsover Parish Church wardens, sidesmen and bellringers in the early 1900s. Back row: Mr. Riley, Frank Wagstaffe, John Flint, Mr. Robbins, Mr. Parsons, Mr. Coupe, Mr. Bemrose (manager of the Waterworks). Front row: Remalia Coupe, Fred Farmer (Churchwarden), Mr. Tatlow (Churchwarden), Ben Norburn, Mr. Coupe.

Bolsover Parish Church bellringers were Derbyshire champions in 1964. Left to right: Robert Chambers, Harold Wagstaffe, Allan Keller, Linda Shaw, Dennis Cooper, Bessie Holmes.

The Duchess of Devonshire samples mouthfuls of ox after trying her hand at roasting it in Sherwood Lodge grounds. The date is 1961 and the event was a fund raising one for the parish church fire restoration fund. Pictured alongside are Councillor Matt Simpson, Councillor L. Revill the Mayor of Bolsover, Rev. W. Speakman. A. Coupe was the butcher.

Carr Vale Evergreen Club in the 1950s, together with an assortment of grandchildren on a trip to Trentham Gardens, Staffordshire.

May Day in 1932 at New Bolsover School, with the castle ranged impressively overhead. Maypole dancing at school has largely died out but in many places it remained an annual feature of school life until the 1960s.

The parade is getting ready, but for what. Was it an early armistice day service? The date is certainly between 1918 and 1921 when the war memorial was erected and events such as this graduated to the old Market Place. The shop names behind are evocative for many of what were for years household names in Bolsover; E. Woodhead and Sons, Public Benefit Boot and Shoe Co., and J. Eyre. Christopher Hinde's house at the end still looks domestic even though by this time half had been converted to commercial use.

Bolsover W.I. perform their 'Ladies of Derbyshire' pageant in the grounds of Sherwood Lodge. The occasion was the golden jubilee of the national federation of W.I.'s in 1965. Among the 'ladies' are Florence Nightingale, Bess of Hardwick and Catherine Mompesson. From the top left: Mesdames, Shaw, Millard, Young, Lenthall, Whitworth, Ashby, Newman, – , Bowler, Taylor, Share, Crofts, Chandler, Lynn, Rhodes, Muggleston, Carter, Howarth, Price, Marriott, Hewitt, Speight.

Ward's charabanc carried Bozerites on their adventurous days out. Mr. Ward was a coal merchant living in what is now Carr Vale Post Office. The vehicle seen here was ingeniously designed so that the passenger top could be removed and replaced with a more suitable one for carrying coal.

King George V and Queen Mary visited Bolsover on June 25 1914 on their way to Welbeck Abbey as guests of the Duke and Duchess of Portland. The top photograph shows the royal couple sitting in the rear of the Daimler and arriving in the Market Place. The bottom one is of the reception committee. Mr. McKay is the man in the trilby hat standing immediately to the right of the lady in the centre. Mr. Overton, colliery official stands directly behind the top hatted gentleman at the front.

At the turn of the century Bolsover maintained a flourishing Orchestral Society. Here they are in 1908, posed in the castle grounds. Back row: J. Burgin, D. Carter, F. Peters, J. Bemrose, H. Moore, W. Shelton, Dr. Stratton (conductor), J. Hogg, A. Hughes, E. Cook, B. Carter, J. Beresford. Middles row: A. Knighton, Mr. Knighton, F. Knighton, J. Shannon, Miss Riley, – , Mr. Turner, A. Knighton, A. Rowland, I. Handford. Front row: G. Thorpe, – , C. Cutts.

Although the composition of this photograph is poor, historically it is of great interest, being the only known photograph of Winifred, Duchess of Portland on a visit to Bolsover, although she was very active locally in opening fetes, galas and church bazaars. The occasion is the laying of the commemorative plaque to St. Winifred's Church, Carr Vale in 1907. The Duchess, wife of the sixth Duke and acknowledged as one of the great beauties of the Edwardian era was famous for her charitable works in the mining communities of north Derbyshire and north Nottinghamshire, earning her the title of the 'Miners Duchess'.

Bolsover Angling Club in 1904. The previous day they had fished at Boston in Lincolnshire.

Councillor Savage, Chairman of Bolsover UDC pictured with Mrs. Savage reading a letter from Decazeville, presented by Madamoiselle Hussin. Mrs. Rita Inns is second left. The photograph was taken in the Elder Citizens Centre, High Street in 1962.

It was in 1955 that Rita Inns first visited Decazeville in southern France with a party of children from Shirebrook grammar school. In 1962 Bolsover UDC became officially 'twinned' with its French counterpart and school exchanges have continued ever since. Here we see Monsieur Rene Rouquette Mayor of Decazeville, Councillor Frank Cross, Chairman of Bolsover UDC and Monsieur Thamié, Deputy Mayor of Decazeville parading through a very wet Market Place, on an official exchange visit in the early 1960s.

Fred Kitchen, best selling novelist of the 1940s and 1950s with such titles as 'Brother to the Ox', 'Life on the Land' and 'The Ploughman Homeward Plods' spent his later years living in Moor Lane, Bolsover. His books are a marvellously accurate and readable fictional account of the life of an agricultural worker in the first half of this century. 'Settlers in England' records life on the Oxcroft settlement in the 1920s. 'Brother to the Ox' was filmed for television in 1981. Fred Kitchen was a hard working self educated man and a sensitive recorder of a life now long gone.

Coronation year 1953 heralded a level of festivities on a local as well as a national scale which it is unlikely will ever be repeated; street parties, bunting, fireworks and a spate of patriotic fervour which has never been equalled since and Bolsover was no exception. Here we see a replica of the Queen's crown being lowered on to its plinth in the Market Place and shops down Station Road alive with bunting, flags, portraits of the Queen and loyal decorations. Today, the Britannic Insurance Company has taken over most of the block.

The two wagonettes transporting this exclusively male outing wait to make their way up Hockley towards the Market Place. The only building remaining today is the red brick house, corner right, which still stands on Station Road, just above the turn off to Old Hill.

Taken outside the old Angel pub Castle Street, before its replacement by the present building. A rather miscellaneous group of men, although two who are recognisable are Jack Coupe and John Henry Adsetts in knee breeches on the front row, He is remembered as being rather 'dressier' than most men in Bolsover at the time.

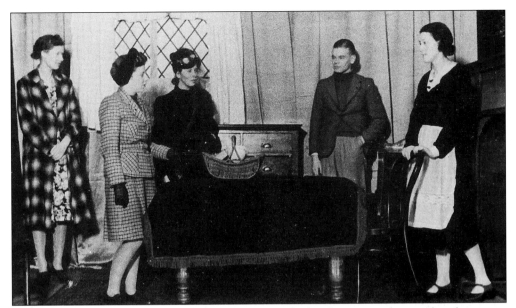

St. Winifred's Church Drama Group was a very popular local group producing plays for twenty years. Its first night in 1940 coincided with the German bombing of Sheffield and between acts members were required for fire watching. The group was self supporting, making all its own costumes and scenery and was popular enough to tour church halls throughout north Derbyshire. 'Vacant Possession' produced in the early 1940s is a one act play. Here we see Freda Houfton, Elsie Bradshaw, Lilian Jennings, Harold Shaw and Phyllis Bird. The final production was Somerset Maugham's 'Sacred Flame' in 1960.

A production of 'Mother Superior' with left to right: Margaret Ogden, Mary Jackson, Phyllis Bird, Jean Proll, Margaret Davidson, Elsie Barker, Anne Williams, Sheila Webster and (behind) Marjorie Chambers and Eunice Ogden. Phyllis Bird recalls her 'Mother Superior' white robe was made from a Victorian nightdress and her girdle from very early nylon parachute cord.

BOLSOVER NATIONAL SCHOOLS.

— A —

GRAND BAZAAR

AND FANCY FAIR,

WILL BE HELD

In the above Schools,

ON

THURSDAY, AUG. 8TH, 1895,

AND THE FOLLOWING MONDAY & WEDNESDAY, AUG. 12th & 14th,

UNDER THE DISTINGUISHED PATRONAGE OF

THE DUKE AND DUCHESS OF PORTLAND.
THE DUKE AND DUCHESS OF DEVONSHIRE.

EARL BATHURST.	LADY BATHURST.
THE BISHOP OF SOUTHWELL	LADY WALKER.
ARCHDEACON FREER.	LADY LAURA RIDDING.
MAJOR HALLOWES.	MRS. HALLOWES.
Dr. COURT.	MRS. COURT.
Dr. GOODWIN SHEA.	MRS. SHEA.
THOS. SHILLITOE, Esq.	MRS. SHILLITOE.
W. BURKITT, Esq., J.P.	MRS. STILWELL.
S. BURKITT, Esq., J.P.	MRS. BURKITT.
W. H. RANGELEY, Esq.	MRS. BYRON.
R. S. HOUSELEY, Esq.	MRS. JACKSON.
Dr. COLE.	MRS. RANGELEY.
Dr. G. BOOTH, J.P.	MRS. WELFITT.
P. H. CHANDLER, Esq., J.P.	MRS. CRIPWELL.
A. W. BYRON, Esq.	MISS MIDWORTH.
Rev. C. P. GOOD.	MRS. R. S. HOUSELEY.

THE PROCEEDS OF WHICH WILL BE DEVOTED TO CLEARING OFF THE DEBT INCURRED IN BUILDING & ENLARGING SHUTTLEWOOD & THE ABOVE SCHOOLS,

The Bazaar and Fancy Fair willbe opened on THURSDAY, August 8th, at 2.30 p.m. by

HER GRACE THE DUCHESS OF PORTLAND,

ACCOMPANIED BY THE DUKE AND FRIENDS.

On MONDAY, Aug. 12th, at 2.30 p.m., by Mrs. JACKSON (Miss Hallowes), of Clay Cross Hall

On WEDNESDAY, August 14th, at 4.30 p.m. by Mrs. GOODWIN SHEA, of Chesterfield.

REFRESHMENTS WILL BE PROVIDED AT MODERATE CHARGES.

In addition to the Sale of Useful and Fancy Articles there will be a series of Entertainments and Amusements.

By the kindness of His Grace the Duke of Portland, Bolsover Castle will be Open to Visitors to the Bazaar. Tickets 3d. each, to be obtained of the Stallholders.

On WEDNESDAY, August 14th, TEA will be provided from 3.30 p.m. Tickets 9d. and 1/- each.

Prices of Admission to Bazaar and Fancy Fair :—On THURSDAY, August 8th, to 4 o'clock, 1s. 6d. ; after 4, 1s. On MONDAY, August 12th, 6d. ; on WEDNESDAY, August 14th, 3d.

Donations and Contributions to the Bazaar will be gratefully received by the Committee, and each day of the Bazaar gifts of eatables will be thankfully received by the Refreshment Stall-holders.

Stall Holders.

1.
Mrs. HILLS
Mrs. TAYLOR
Mrs. SIMKEN
Mrs. GILROY
Miss KNIGHTON

2.
Mrs. STILWELL
Mrs. SHILLITOE
Mrs. SHEA
Miss RAYNER

3.
Mrs. TINSLEY
Mrs. PALMER
Mrs. CALOW
Misses REVILL
Mrs. NORMAN

4.—FLOWER STALL.
Mrs. WEST
Mrs. SCORER
The Misses OAKEY, TAYLOR, HAYWOOD, and JENKINSON

5.—CAKE STALL.
Mrs. HUNTER
Mrs. RHODES

6.—BIBLE CLASS.
Mrs. HARDWICK
Mrs. BANNER
Mrs. THORNLEY
Mr. GEO. MYCOCK

7.—REFRESHMENTS.
Mrs. BAGSHAWE
Mrs. HARKER
Mrs. COOK
Mrs. MARPLES
Mrs. F. HOUFTON
Miss ADSETTS
Mr. OGDEN

8.—TOBACCO STALL.
Miss SIMKEN
  „ EVELYN SIMKEN
  „ CARSON

9.—SHUTTLEWOOD STALL
Mrs. and Miss METTAM
Mrs. FOGERTY
Miss EDITH NICHOLSON

10.—TEACHERS' STALL.
Misses VAUGHAN, PYATT, MARSH, JOHNSON, STEVENSON, and HOOD

11.—VICARAGE SEWING MEETING STALL.
Mrs. HUSBAND
The Misses JUST, BENNETT, and HALL

12.—BRAN TUB.
No. 1.—Master PAUL GILROY
No. 2.—Master LIONEL TAYLOR

13.—SWEET STALL.
Misses M. & E. TWIDLE

Order of Proceedings.

On THURSDAY, August 8th,

The Children will assemble outside the Schools, and sing on the approach of the Duke and Duchess.

Introduction of School Managers, Bazaar Committee and tenantry to the Duke and Duchess.

The Band will play as the Duchess enters the room.

Presentation of a Bouquet to the Duchess, by Miss Dolly Shillitoe.

OBJECT OF THE BAZAAR BRIEFLY EXPLAINED BY THE VICAR.

Bolsover Cycling Club in 1935.

Bolsover Division of the St. John's Ambulance Brigade was formed in July 1910. The colliery schools became the Division H.Q. and each member subscribed towards his own uniform at one shilling per week. Two world wars saw many ambulancemen away fighting and at home on air raid precaution duties. More recent years have seen the Bolsover Division as winners of many national trophies. Here we see an early class held in the castle grounds.

In the shadow of the castle and New Bolsover model village, Lady Edwina Mountbatten reviews members of Bolsover Colliery Ambulance Division on 18 September 1955.

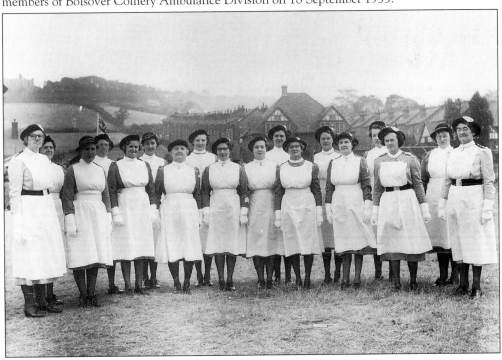

Collieries have always taken great pride in their brass or silver bands. Here we see members of the Bolsover Colliery Silver Prize Band outside the colliery offices and (below) marching along High Street outside the Pearce Trust bungalows.

Bolsover Colliery Cricket Club in 1920. The Houfton Cup was presented by Mr. John Plowright Houfton at this time General manager of the Bolsover Colliery Company and a keen cricketer. The Company was very keen on sporting activities for its workforce, encouraging not only cricket but football, mens' hockey, tennis and bowls teams to flourish.

Josie James stands on the chequer board, a draught board patch which for many years stood in the Hornscroft.

Proud owners with their decorated floats and horses pose in the Hornscroft following a flower day parade.

First Hillstown Derbyshire Boys Brigade 1937/38. First row: Dennis Revill, Keith Yapp, George Bratt, Eric Storbrook, Eric Mawby. Second row: Louis Lawday, Ian Smith, Gordon Simms, George Young, Alan Stephenson, Henry Bennett, Alan Revill. Third row: Cyril Alsop, Irvine Waterfall, John Price, George Chamberlain, Ivan Beresford, Edmund Smith. Fourth row: Maurice Leaning, Desmond Stephens, Douglas Beresford, Ray Kemp, Percy Edwards, Alan Attenborough. Taken outside the Methodist Chapel.

The unveiling of the war memorial in the Market Place in 1921 by Mr. C.A. Cochrane, Chairman of the Bolsover Colliery Company Ltd. Costs were met by public subscription and the design executed by Sir Reginald Blomfield who decided that a replica of the Imperial War Cross set up in military cemeteries throughout northern France after the Great War was most appropriate. Known as the 'Cross of Sacrifice' it has inscribed on it the names of 175 men and women of Bolsover and Hillstown who lost their lives during the first war. After 1945 further names were added.

Bolsover Jazz Band outside the Blue Bell.

The quality of the photograph is not good but it does illustrate how in the nineteenth century events like the annual flower show involved almost the whole town. Hundreds took part through church and chapel sunday schools, Miners Welfares and Institutes. The decorated farm carts and drays piled high with flowers and children offer some indication of the sheer colour and enthusiasm of the participants who assembled here in the Market Place, later making their way to the castle.

This decorated horse and cart stands outside Town End Chapel. Arthur Harold Coupe is also in his Sunday best.

A nineteenth century view of Palterton Hall, built in the 1740s by Richard Milnes of Chesterfield although its status had changed from hall to farmhouse by the time this photograph was taken. A very striking building as it peers west across the Vale of Scarsdale and the Doe Lea valley.

Palterton post office when it was situated along Orchard Terrace before moving to Back Lane. The letter box was conveniently placed in the front window so the post master could retrieve letters easily; what a target this would be today for the prospective vandal! The public notices dated 1909 include 'lost, black silk umbrella' and a swine fever revocation notice.

This small thatched cottage with its bedroom window almost enclosed under the eaves was known as 'Wilcockson's Cottage'. It was tucked away under the hill below St. Lukes Mission Church.

Mrs. Ludlam at the door of her shop in Scotland Yard. The shop itself was a former house parlour and the window a glorious combination reflecting the necessities of the time; stock powder, mint humbugs, socks and cleaning materials.

The first Hare and Hounds village pub. Originally three separate cottages it later moved to a flat roofed 1930s building on the edge of the village. The new pub finally closed in 1993.

Highfields Farm in 1940. Unusual as the long arm of the building would appear to be single storey while the gable end at the same roof level has two.

This group of ladies was taken outside Palterton school shortly before the first world war. The event was the opening of the school and the group we see here had provided the tea.

Six
Shuttlewood

St. Lawrence's Church, taken at the time of the opening of the new vestries in 1909. Built in 1893 as a village school and mission church on land given by the Duke of Portland and money provided by the Vicar of Bolsover Rev. T.C. Hills it originally comprised two rooms. In 1907 on the opening of the new school building it became known as St. Lawrence's Church.

Infants class and Standards II and III taken in 1899.

Shuttlewood teachers in the early years of this century; Mrs. James, Mrs. Skelton, Mrs Woodward and Mrs. Fogerty, Headmistress. Between 1894 and 1993 the school has only had six head teachers. The background tiles are there to this day!

Cutting through the 'new road' between Shuttlewood and Stanfree in 1905. The buildings to the right of the road are the Oxcroft colliery offices. The horsedrawn trucks containing the aggregate ran on rails up the incline towards the Travellers Rest pub.

Sunny Bank cottages at Stanfree stood at the top of Long Lane which ran between Shuttlewood and Stanfree. They were demolished in 1963.

Only the pantiled porch tells us this is not a Scottish crofter's cottage. Unusually for Derbyshire this Shuttlewood dwelling was thatched. Nearby stood a pond in which watercress flourished, eagerly gathered by villagers when in season.

Shuttlewood Church Lads Brigade taken about 1910.

Shuttlewood Infants School in 1928. The youthful looking teacher is Miss Cooke. At the time the school buildings were an excellent example of local authority educational provision.

Bole Appleton farm Shuttlewood still stands today on its ridge overlooking the Doe Lea valley. When this was taken the farm was fairly isolated but in the 1930s and 1940s this side of Shuttlewood Road was gradually infilled with ribbon development connecting the village with Bolsover.

Shuttlewood school teachers in the 1890s. Mrs. E.A. Fogerty seated left was headmistress from 1894 to 1924.

Seven
Carr Vale and New Bolsover

Station Master Bluff, complete with magnificent beard at Carr Vale Station.

Scenes from the flood of July 1912 when, after an unusually heavy rain storm water poured off the escarpment, down the Bolsover tunnel and into Carr Vale. Marsden's and the Coronation Bazaar stood in Main Street opposite the Carr Vale Hotel. Miners home from the shift were given the task of damming the water channel down the centre of Main Street and Charlesworth Street into the Doe Lea.

Main Street 27 July 1912
Carr Vale
After Cloud Burst

Teaching staff at the colliery schools, New Bolsover. Standing left to right: Miss Jenkinson, Mrs. Toomey, Mrs. Cooper, Miss Godfrey, Miss Merryweather. Seated left to right: Tom Piper, Miss Mole, Mr. Wigglesworth (Headmaster), Mrs. Alsop, Mr. Alsop.

A car progresses up Main Street, Carr Vale, admired by the rather puzzled looking miners standing in front of a very finely decorated Carr Vale Hotel. It is uncertain whether the occasion was the visit to Bolsover of King George V and Queen Mary in 1914 or the Armistice Day Celebrations four years later.

Bolsover colliery club and institute is an attractive building possessing a generalised arts and crafts feel. Situated at the centre of the model village, opposite cricket ground and bowling green, today it offers a more generous measure of drink than in its early days when miners were restricted to 'no more than three glasses between 6 pm and 10 pm'.

St. Winifred's does not commemorate the actual Saint but Winifred, Duchess of Portland, wife of the sixth Duke. The Duke's half sister Lady Ottoline Morrell was a great enthusiast of Bolsover castle and her mother was created Baroness Bolsover in 1880. Today, St. Winifred's houses Castle Lane Motors and the Duchess is remembered by a stone plaque on the outside wall.

The colliery schools building was a magnificent looking building, overlooking the green and completing the village development to the west. Built in red brick with bays, gables and a central tower it is very evocative of early twentieth century model villages built elsewhere. Lord Leverhulme's Port Sunlight and the later Cadbury development at Bournville are closely related architecturally to the colliery schools. Six classrooms ran down either side of a central hall which was covered by a hammer beam roof. The Bolsover Colliery Company was Liberal nonconformist in outlook and not keen on having miners' children educated in the Church of England school in the old village. They refused the vicar of Bolsover's request for a grant of £500 in order to extend 'his' school and instead built their own. When its school function ceased the building was used as the village hall. Unfortunately a very popular local campaign to convert it into a sports and leisure centre was unsuccessful and the building was demolished in 1987.

The Cooperative Stores, a branch of the Pleasley and Pleasley Hill Society was a very important feature of the model village. It was the only shop in the immediate vicinity although nearby Carr Vale possessed a wide range of shops. The Stores itself was designed with separate departments for boots, groceries, drapery and butchery. It was planned on the assumption that there would be two hundred trading members of the Society. Exactly the number of houses within the village. The aim was that the Stores would hold a virtual monopoly on trade within New Bolsover. In a letter to Emerson Bainbridge, Chairman of the Bolsover Colliery Company, John Plowright Houfton the Colliery manager regrets that it has not been possible to exclude from the village the local travelling draper. Each family had to take out at least a £1 share in the Cooperative which also included a cooperative piggery containing twenty to thirty pigs.

Bolsover was part of the Great Central Railway for main line services, with a station at the foot of Station Road. The Lancashire, Derbyshire and East Coast Railway ran through Carr Vale towards Scarcliffe and a network of mineral lines connected pits throughout the Derbyshire and Nottinghamshire coalfield. Here we see the Great Central Railway station before the Great War.

Carr Vale crossing was the scene of various fatalities earlier this century. The pedestrian gates, unlike the rail ones, were always open and children were especially vulnerable. One died in 1909, three in 1910 and another in 1923. The clarity of this photograph recaptures the era wonderfully.

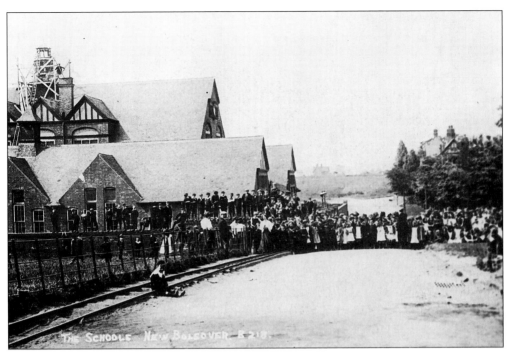

It is uncertain exactly why all the schoolchildren from the colliery schools at New Bolsover should be ranged across the road between village and school. Can it really be for this particular photograph. And why has one little lad escaped to sit on the tub railway? This ran between the colliery and the backs of the cottages, serving a dual purpose; delivering house coal and removing night soil.

Outside Ginnevers shop, Charlesworth Street, Carr Vale. The building is now Carr Vale post office.

CARR VALE SECOND FLOOD
AUG 26ᵗʰ 1912

1912 was obviously a very wet and unfortunate year for Carr Vale for at the end of August a second flood affected the village by way of the Bolsover tunnel and the railway line. However, it did provide an excellent photograph of the station seen here when use of the railway was at its height.

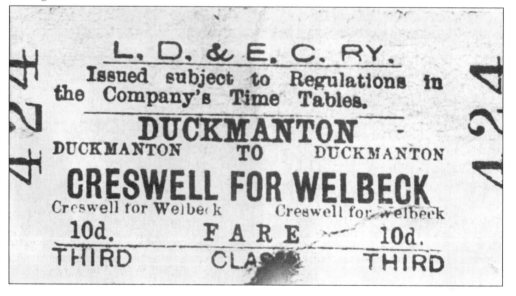

424

L. D. & E. C. RY.

Issued subject to Regulations in the Company's Time Tables.

DUCKMANTON   -

DUCKMANTON   TO   DUCKMANTON

CRESWELL FOR WELBECK

Creswell for Welbeck   Creswell for Welbeck

10d.   FARE   10d.

THIRD   CLASS   THIRD

424

Bolsover Colliery School football team 1928–29. Staff: Mr. Miller, Mr. Haddock (Headmaster), Mr. Hollis. Back row: T. Bluff, C. Riley, F. Dexter, N. Madin, G. Allock, M. Needham. Front row: F. Pickard, A. Wood, W. Pilkington, W. Millard, I. Davis, B. Roberts.

The Wesleyan chapel at New Bolsover, built for the model village and taken soon after its opening in 1905. Bainbridge Hall, then an orphanage stands alongside.

Arthur Harold Coupe with his son Oscar and daughters Eva and Cynthia seen here in their garden at Orchard Row, Carr Vale, together with a multitude of rabbits.

An excellent view of the viaduct which carried the Lancashire, Derbyshire and East Coast Railway on its way towards the Bolsover tunnel. The mineral line running underneath ran from Bolsover Colliery to Glapwell, Rowthorne and Pleasley pits.

Eight
Work and Worship

THE BOLSOVER PARISH MAGAZINE.

BAPTIZED.

" One Lord, one Faith, one Baptism,"

August 25th, Albert, son of Richard and Sarah Tonks.

,, ,, Richard, son of Richard and Sarah Tonks.

,, ,, Beatrice, daughter of Richard and Sarah Tonks.

,, ,, Priscilla, daughter of John and Ruth Millward.

Sept. 15th, Winifred Hannah, daughter of John Robert and Elizabeth Evans.

,, 22nd, Dorothy, daughter of Arthur Frederick and Maybel Houfton.

,, 25th, Joseph William, son of Harry and Emily Clark.

,, ,, Annie Mary, daughter of Henry Arthur and Ada Cutts.

,, ,, Margaret Ann, daughter of Joseph and Jane Barton.

,, ,, Edmund Alfred, son of Alfred and Nellie Flecknell.

,, 27th, John, son of James and Mary Bates.

,, 29th, Ethel, daughter of Rufus and Jane Firth.

,, ,, Charlotte Johnson, daughter of Thomas and Emma Chadburn.

October 2nd, Horace Harry, son of Jonah and Mary Eliza Shepherd.

,, 4th, John Arthur, son of John and Mary Yates.

,, 6th, Eric, son of James and Annie Eliza Wright.

,, 9th, Frances, daughter of Thomas and Mary Cuttell.

,, ,, Frances, daughter of John and Lilly Mountney.

,, ,, John Edward, son of John and Elizabeth Cree.

,, 13th, Albert Edwin, son of Henry and Mary Bailey.

,, 16th, Elsie Mary, daughter of Alfred and Mary Elizabeth Garbett.

,, ,, Blanche Gertrude, daughter of William and Mary Frith.

,, ,, Maggie, daughter of William and Mary Frith.

,, ,, Harold, son of Frank and Ellen Sales.

October 21st, John, son of John and Elizabeth Murden.

,, 23rd, Francis William, son of William and Janet Coupe.

,, ,, Ethel, daughter of Jesse and Annie Bradley.

,, ,, Annie, daughter of Daniel and Eliza Newton.

,, ,, Elsie May, daughter of William and Sarah Presley.

,, ,, Joseph Willoughby, son of Robert and Mary Hannah Allen.

✻   ✻   ✻

MARRIED.

" Signifying unto us the mystical union that is betwixt Christ and His Church."

Sept. 26th, John William Ogden and Priscilla Wyatt.

,, ,, James Fielding and Marinah Rodgers.

October 6th, Samuel Turner and Eliza Ann Bond.

,, 24th, John Fletcher and Charlotte Bennett.

✻   ✻   ✻

BURIED.

" I am the Resurrection and the Life."

July 19th, Thomas Maxfield, aged 62 years.
,, 21st, Albert Bailey, aged 4 years.
,, 26th, Thomas Caulton, aged 9 months.
,, 28th, Alfred Devney, aged 8 months.
,, 29th, William Taylor, aged 12 months.
,, 31st, Minnie Russell, aged 7 months.
Oct. 2nd, John Bates, aged 6 months.
,, ,, Percy Sydney Smith, aged 3 months.
,, 3rd, Robert Hitchcock, aged 55 years.
,, 8th, Arthur Fairbrother, aged 2 years.
,, ,, John Arthur Yates, aged 2 years.
,, 9th, Thomas Rees Morris, aged 15 years.
,, ,, Jack Bradley, aged 1 year.
,, 15th, Mary Johnson, aged 72 years.
,, ,, John Joseph Camp, aged 18 months.
,, 16th, Sarah Hannah Flint, aged 10 years.
,, 17th, Beatrice Tonks, aged 21 months.

The Bolsover parish church magazine for 1895 records not only baptisms and marriages but the very sad fact that out of seventeen deaths between July and October a staggering fourteen of these were children.

The Primitive Methodist Church was a fine example of nineteenth century nonconformist architecture in the best 'no nonsense' chapel tradition. Spacious and dominant on its Town End site, like many of its kind it became too large for a dwindling congregation and was demolished in 1974. The Wesleyan methodists at Trinity then merged with the 'Prims' to meet in the Hill Top Church.

The Primitive Methodist Church, Town End in 1900. John Askey to the left with twenty two of his scholars. He was a founder member and on his right is the foundation stone laid by him. John came to Bolsover, as did so many others, from the Peak District lead mines to raise the coal. His daughter Nelly is third left on the second row.

A marvellously atmospheric shot of Bolsover Colliery in its pre second world war heyday. Heavy industry at its most dramatic; a world now vanished in Britain.

Welbeck Road Boys School football team 1947–48. The school is now Welbeck Hall of Bolsover school.

109

Bolsover Colliery after its closure in 1994. This was the first of the Bolsover Company's pits to be sunk, coal being reached in 1891. Bolsover was regarded as the 'Rolls Royce' of companies with progressive housing and social policies towards its workforce and forward in mining developments. The disadvantage was that this all round control led to a lack of individual freedom for miners and their families when education, leisure, religion, housing and employment were all provided by the company. Bolsover was not as productive as the company's later 'Dukeries' pits. For many years after nationalisation Bolsover was the HQ for the North Derbyshire Area of the NCB.

Outside the machine shop at Glapwell colliery in 1919 are three members of the Coupe family of Bolsover. First left on the back row is Alfred Coupe and William second from the right. Front centre is Arthur Askey Coupe who was well known in Bolsover until his death, aged ninety, in 1993. After working at Glapwell all three transferred to Oxcroft colliery. Arthur Coupe began work at the pit aged thirteen.

The depression years of the 1930s saw terrible poverty and despair among working class communities and the coalfield areas were no exception. Here we see the Hillstown Relief Committee in the process of allocating soup and bread rations.

Members of the Welbeck Road school soup kitchen staff including the headmaster Mr. Day. Soup and bread was rationed out to hungry children and their families.

These four photographs show the devastation caused by the fire which ripped through the parish church in 1897. Miraculously the tower and the Cavendish Chapel remained relatively unscathed but the body of the church was left in a ruinous and roofless state. They record the terrible damage the fire inflicted and work in progress towards rebuilding.

Masons, carpenters and building workers with Rev. T.C. Hills and curate outside the shell of the parish church during rebuilding work following the 1897 fire.

The first venue for methodist worship in the mining village of New Bolsover was the colliery schools but on September 7 1904, Emerson Bainbridge, Chairman of the Bolsover Colliery Company helped lay the first memorial stones and included a tea for the villagers. Six months later this Wesleyan church was opened. Of the £2,100 needed, £500 came from the company. Sadly this fine chapel, situated adjacent to the orphanage, on the corner of Chapel Road and New Station Road was demolished in the early 1980s.

'Who is on the Lord's side? Who will serve the King!' This 1910 parish church calendar almost demands to know.

The carbonisation plant was opened by the Duke of Kent in 1937. Today it is split into two distinct areas; the smokeless fuels plant and the chemicals division utilising by products from the smokeless fuel side. Today, the plant and its emissions raise wide spread environmental concern not only at local but at national level.

The cottages to the rear of men and horses are still there but changed out of all recognition today, with dormer windows and a raised roof line. The group of three stand below Caxton House Hockley, at the far end of the 'brek' between Station Road and Hill Top.

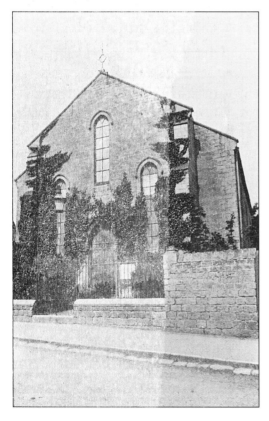

This was the second home for Wesleyan methodists in the town. The first building, sited at the foot of 'Castle Brek' was proving too small by the mid nineteenth century so in 1866 this building with seating for two hundred and fifty was opened. An adjoining school room was added in 1873. Today, the building minus ivy, wall and railings has taken on a new lease of life in the community as the Assembly Hall.

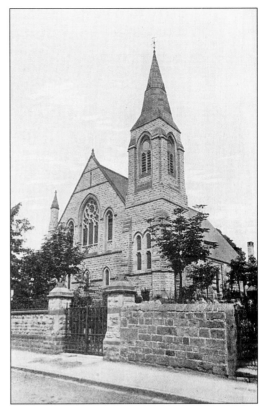

Thirty years later this building replaced the 1866 chapel. The site, on land adjoining Sherwood Lodge, was given by Abel Sykes J.P. and board member of the Bolsover Colliery Company. The building, which seated five hundred people, cost £3,500 and was opened in 1897. Today, Hill Top Methodist Church is 'open plan' minus wall and gate. In 1993 a large side extension commemorating Abel Sykes was opened.

Can anyone recognise this scene? It is thought to have been taken following a fire at the Limekiln Fields Mill. The mill remains but the interior workings have been removed.

A decorated cart, the property of Mr. Eyre, boot and show dealer, stands outside Woodhead's grocers shop. The flowers are for the coronation of King George V and Queen Mary in 1910.

Mr. Stanley Hope, undertaker, in traditional funeral dress. Taken outside his High Street premises in the early 1950s.

The sorry spectacle of the parish church fire of 1897 was re-enacted again in 1960. Here we see a dramatic photograph of the fire at its height, with firemen scaling the roof timbers, followed by a later sad inspection of the internal damage.

Markham No. 2 pit headstocks, taken at a time when steam was paramount in the engine house.

This Cotton Street building has a chequered history. It was built as the first Primitive Methodist Chapel in the town, later used by the Salvation Army and in 1911 became council offices. In 1948 council functions transferred to Sherwood Lodge and this building became the Bolsover branch of the county library. In 1976 with the erection of the new library it reverted back to its council function as offices for Old Bolsover Town Council.

Council workmen in 1930, towards the top of the Hillstown water tower at a time when the ferro concrete structure was nearing completion. It replaced the storage tanks, also at Hillstown, and doubled the capacity of water held to 150,000 gallons. Another ten years was to lapse before the water treatment plant at Whaley Moor was completed.

The first methodist chapel in Hillstown was a stable, rented from a local farmer at two shillings per week. Worshippers renovated it by levelling floors and whitewashing walls. Three years after the first service a piece of land on Langwith Road was purchased and the mission church seating one hundred was built. It was opened on August 20 1902.

Members and officers of Bolsover UDC pay a visit to inspect a public authority housing development. On the front row is Councillor Revill, Miss Tranter (later Mrs. Jack Spray), Councillor Spray, G. Fisher, S. Jennings, Mrs. Jennings, Mrs. Savage. On the back row is Councillor Bluff, Mr. and Mrs. Drake, Charles Margerrison, Mrs. Fisher. Bunty Margerrison, Bill Savage, Katie Aldern, Sid and Hetty Fisher.

The Bolsover strike paying committee pictured during the general strike of 1926 comprised miners and colliery officials. As was common elsewhere during the strike miners gathered coal from the tip in hand carts, barrows and prams; whatever could be pushed and capable of carrying coal. Pictured here are Mr. Overton colliery official, W. Spray, Joe Lakin, Mr. Wastnage, Sam Grainger, Mr. Groves, Mr. Peach, Mr. Lee and Mr. Whiting.